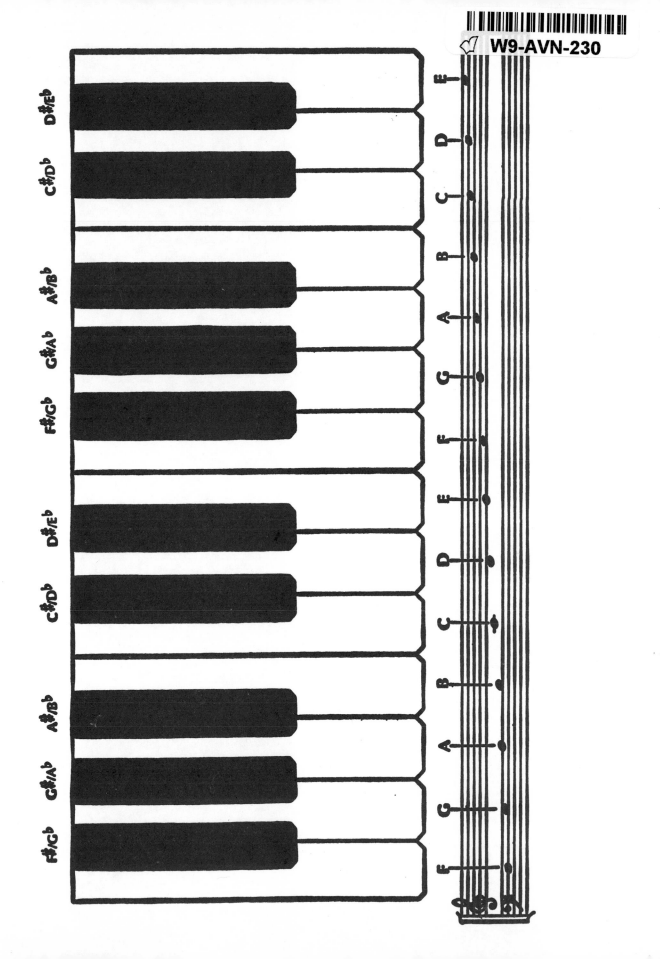

THE Music CONNECTION

SILVER BURDETT GINN

PROGRAM AUTHORS

Jane Beethoven
Dulce Bohn
Patricia Shehan Campbell
Carmen E. Culp
Jennifer Davidson
Lawrence Eisman
Sandra Longoria Glover
Charlotte Hayes

Martha Hilley
Mary E. Hoffman
Sanna Longden
Hunter March
Bill McCloud
Janet Montgomery
Marvelene Moore
Catherine Nadon-Gabrion

Mary Palmer
Carmino Ravosa
Mary Louise Reilly
Will Schmid
Carol Scott-Kassner
Jean Sinor
Sandra Stauffer
Judith Thomas

RECORDING PRODUCERS

Darrell Bledsoe
Jeanine Levenson

J. Douglas Pummill
Buryl Red, Executive Producer

Linda Twine
Ted Wilson

Scott Foresman

Editorial Offices: Glenview, IL • Parsippany, NJ • New York, NY
Sales Offices: Reading, MA • Duluth, GA • Glenview, IL
Carrollton, TX • Menlo Park, CA

ISBN 0-382-34500-2

3 4 5 6 7 8 9 10 - QW - 08 07 06 05 04 03 02 01 00

C·O·N·T

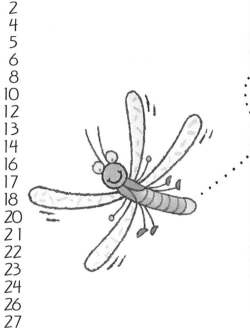

·E·N·T·S

READING

REFERENCE BANK

ump-

A-

A-

eedle

2

In My Feet

eedle

Bump

5

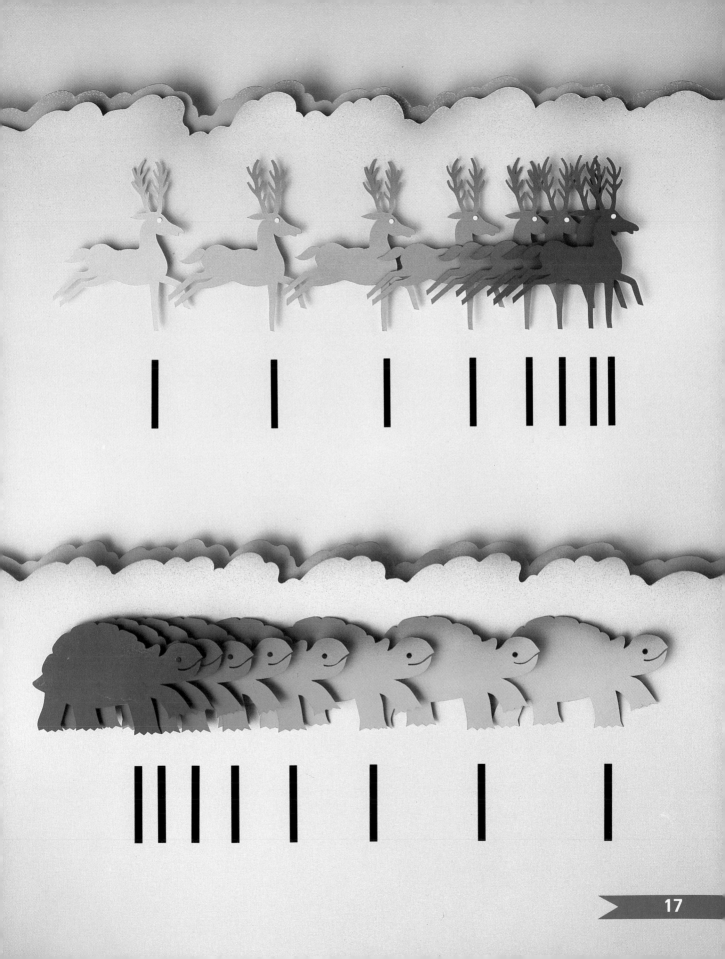

It rained a mist

Man with a Green Beard by Karl Schmidt–Rottluff

Aaron by Thomas Hart Benton

25

I Sing Through the Day

Cock - a - doo - dle, doo - dle, doo.

Whispers of Wishes

Sounds of All My Friends

'Round and 'round, we must go,

Sally Walker (Detail)   by Brenda Joysmith

Medicine Dancers by Cecil Youngfox

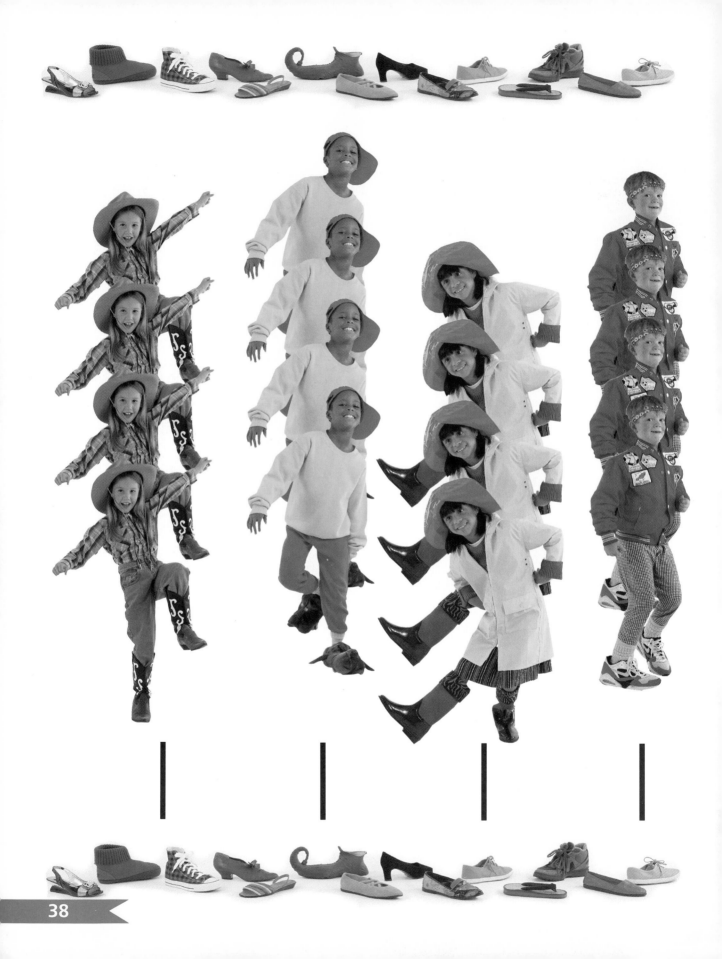

I got a house in Bal - ti - more,

Brus-sels car-pet on the floor,

I got a house in Bal - ti - more,

Street-car runs right by my door,

Deer and Maple Tree, c. 1810   Mori Shushin Tessan

A Piece of Silly Pie

1. eyes
2. nose
3. ears
4. voice
5. fingers
6. toes

44

I like to **eat**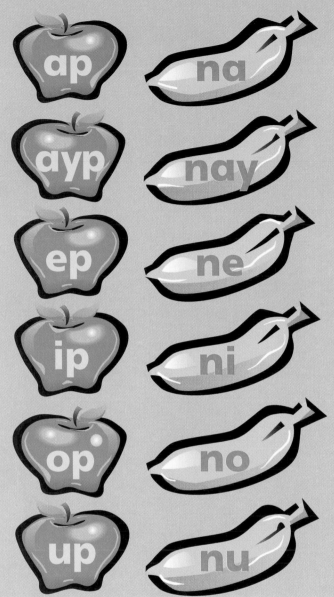

I like to **ate**

I like to **ete**

I like to **ite**

I like to **ote**

I like to **ute**

I like to eat.

Going to a Concert

Songs to End Our Day

Ay-lye, lyu-lye

CD 5-21

Yiddish Folk Song English Words by Richard Morris

Ay - lye, lyu - lye, lyu - lye,

Go to sleep now, don't cry;

Close your eyes in slum - ber,

Oh, my dar - ling kind' - lach.

A Book Is a Magic Carpet

African Noel

CD 6-25, 26

Liberian Folk Song   *Collected and Translated by Aden G. Lewis*

Sing   No - el,   sing   No - el,

Fine

No - el,   No - el. _____

Sing   No - el,   sing   No - el,

D.C. al Fine

No - el,   No - el. _____

The Nutcracker

I'm gonna wrap myself
  in

I'm gonna daub myself
  with

Stick some
  on top of my head,

I'm gonna mail myself
  to you.

I'm a–gonna tie me up in a

I'm gonna tie too;

I'm a–gonna climb up in my

I'm gonna mail myself to you.

Words and music by Woody Guthrie

Footprints and Shadows

Touch the Beat

Engine, Engine

How Many Sounds on a Beat?

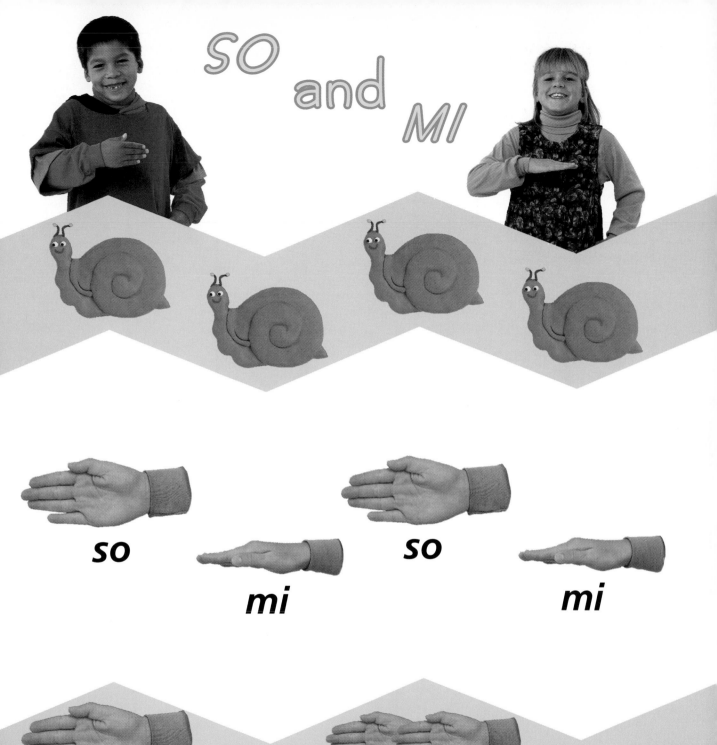

SO and MI

so

mi

so

mi

SO

mi

so   so

mi

Can You Find It ?

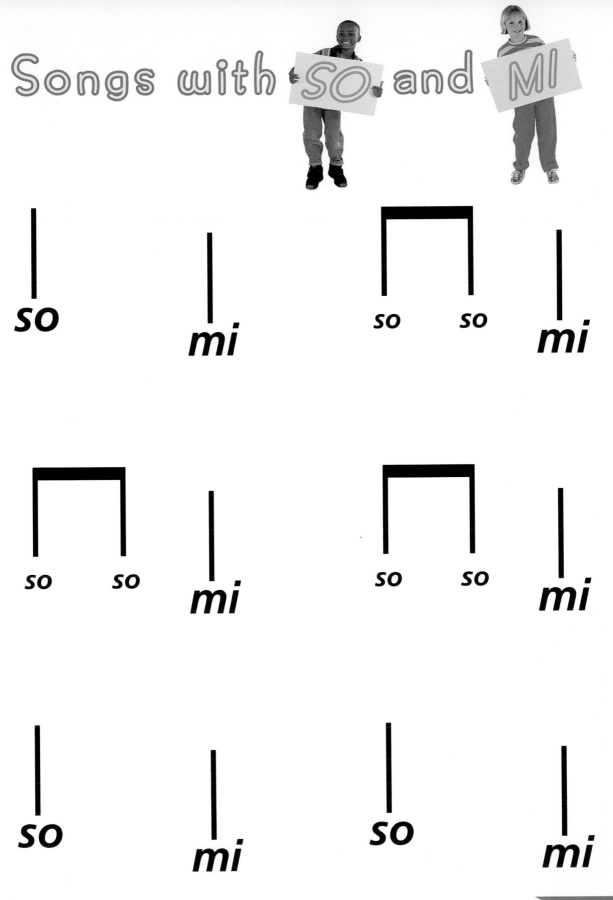

so   mi   so   so   mi

so   so   mi   so   so   mi

so   mi   so   mi

Lines and Spaces

Line 5
Line 4
Line 3
Line 2
Line 1

Space 4
Space 3
Space 2
Space 1

Writing Stems

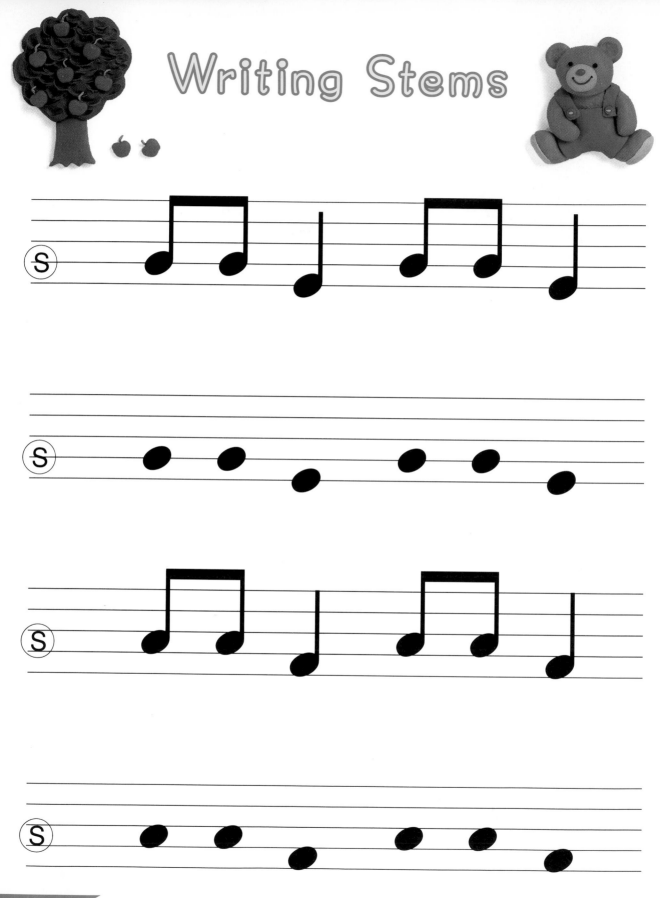

Stems That Go Down

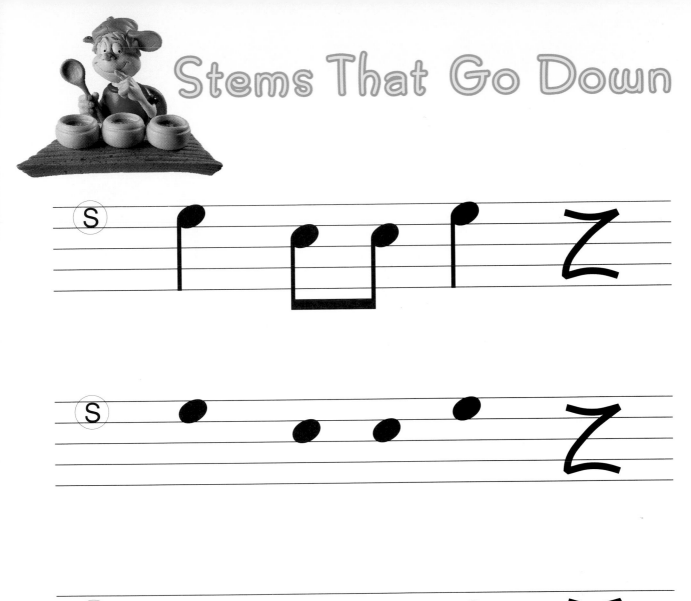

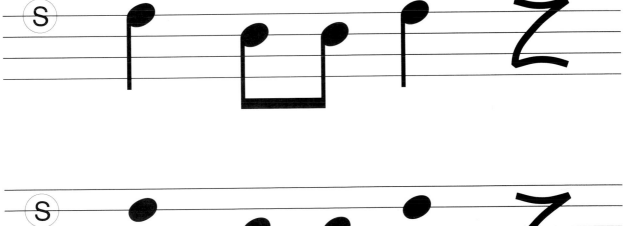

Singing and Playing Melodies

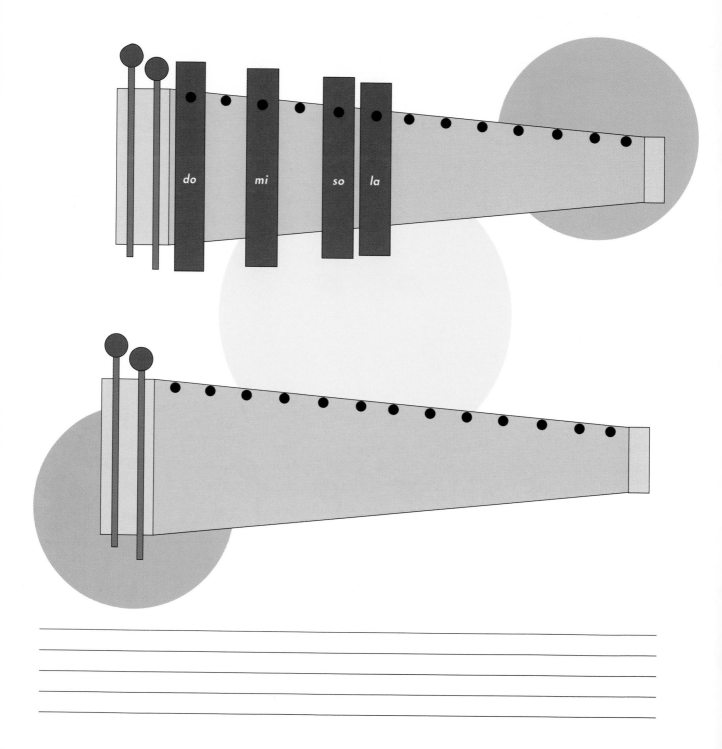

Using *SO, MI,* and ?

Finding a New Note

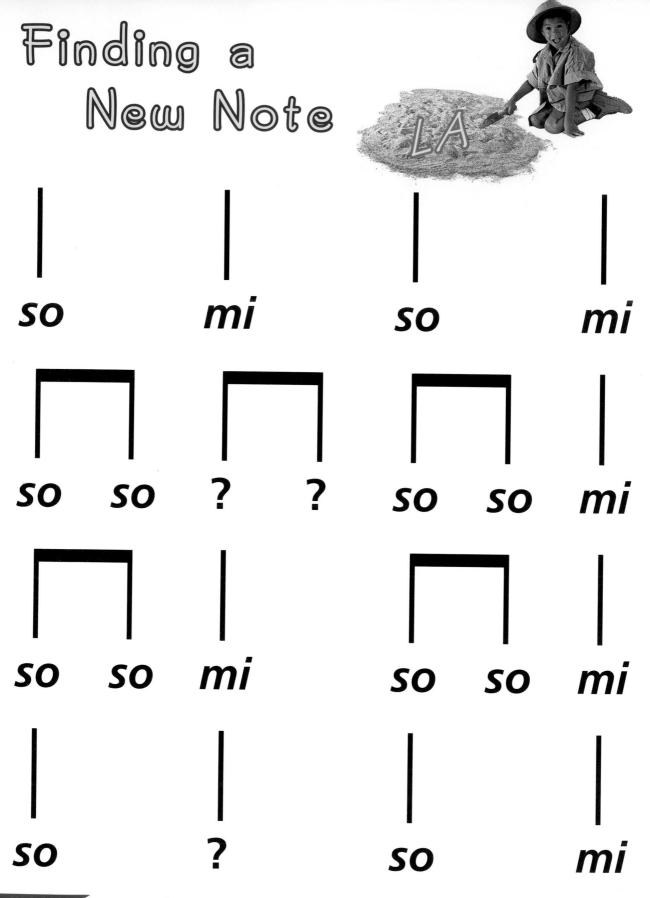

Stems For *SO, MI,* and *LA*

Conducting in Two

A Rhythm Game

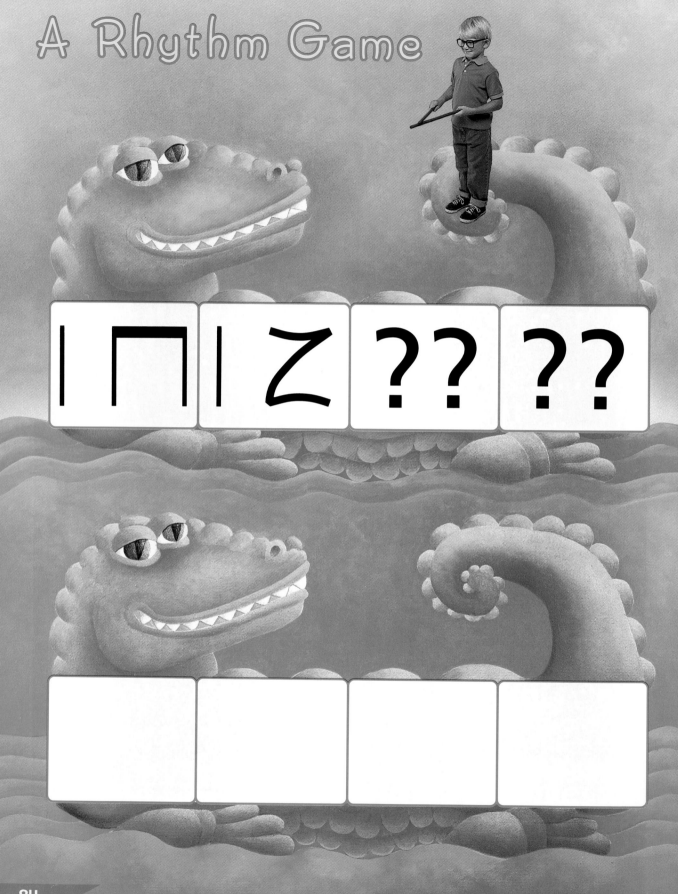

The *SO, MI, DO* Family

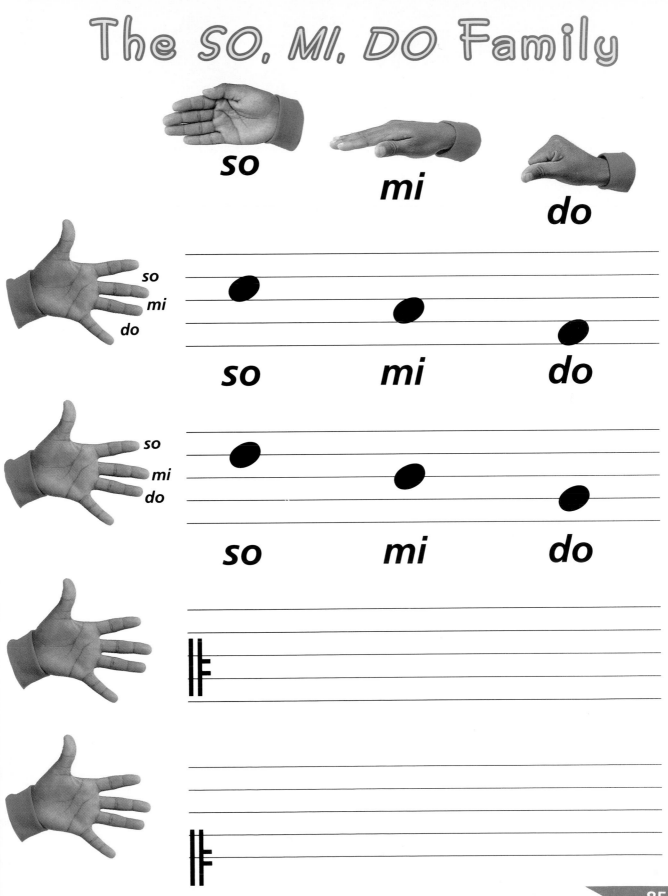

so

mi

do

so
mi
do

so   mi   do

so
mi
do

so   mi   do

Ledger Lines

Little Black Bug

CD 7-50

Music by Ruth Boshkoff   Words by Margaret Wise Brown

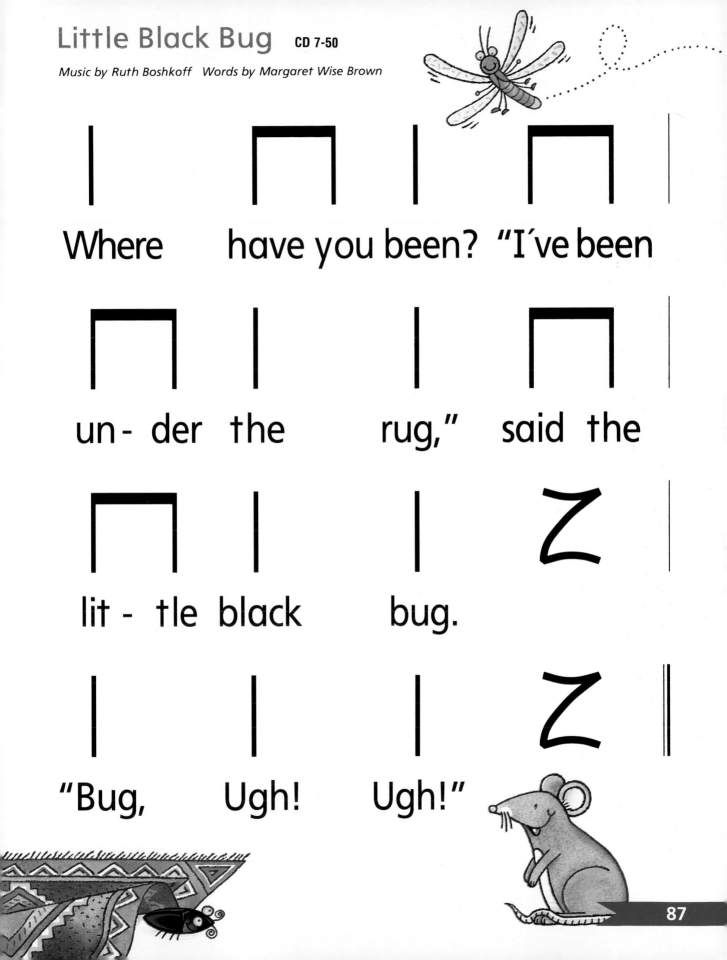

Where   have you been? "I've been

un- der the   rug,"   said the

lit - tle black   bug.

"Bug,   Ugh!   Ugh!"

On a Log, Mister Frog   CD 7-16

Traditional

On a log, Mis - ter Frog,

sang his song the whole day long,

Glumf, glumf, glumf, glumf.

Collected and adapted by Katalin Forrai and Jean Sinor

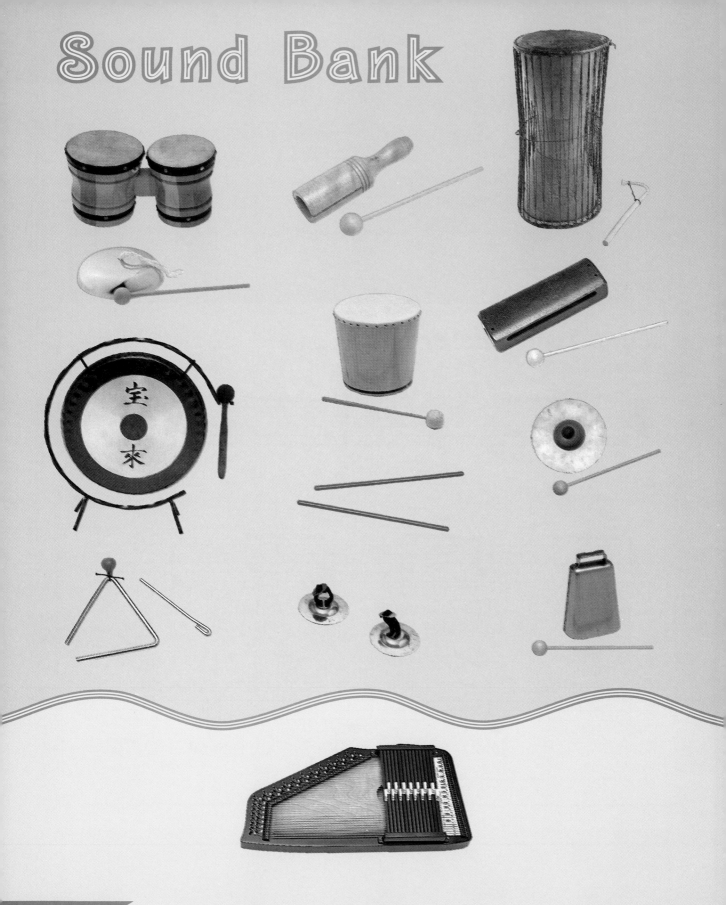

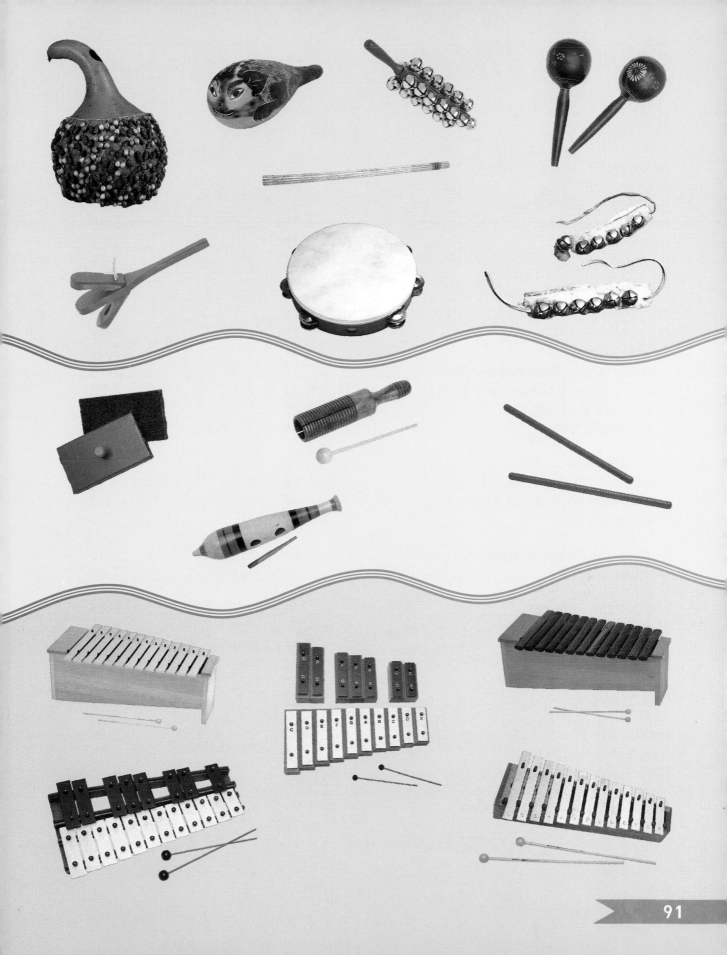

Song Index

	BIG BOOK/ STUDENT TEXT	CD-TRACK NUMBER
Jean, Jean (Chant)	68, 70	7-9
John the Rabbit	27	2-40
Li'l Liza Jane	39	4-2
Listen to the Water	42	4-13
Little Black Bug	87	7-50
Little Green Frog, The	27	2-41
Long Way Home, A	40	4-4
Lucy Locket	73, 81	7-23
Mail Myself to You	64	6-34
Miss White Had a Fright (Chant)	72	7-17
Morning on the Farm	27	3-2
My Owlet	56	5-19
Noble Duke of York	46	4-25
On a Log, Mister Frog	72, 88, 89	7-16
Pease Porridge Hot	74, 77	7-26
Punchinella	38	3-37
Rain, Rain	68, 70, 72, 83	7-10
Rosie, Darling Rosie	22	2-22
'Round and 'Round	36	3-26
Russian Slumber Song	57, 58	1-18
Seesaw	73	7-13
Snail, Snail	71-74, 80	7-7
Spaceworms	50	5-4
Teddy Bear	72, 73, 76, 79, 80	7-19
This Old Man	24, 25	2-32
Time to Sing	30	3-12
When the Saints Go Marching In	8	1-17

Photograph and Illustration Credits

Acknowledgements

Every effort has been made to locate all copyright holders of materials used in this book. If any errors or omissions have occurred, corrections will be made.

Photograph and Illustration Credits

All photographs are by Silver Burdett Ginn (SBG) unless otherwise noted.

Cover: Dralene "Red" Hughes

2-3: Mary Thelen. 3: *r.* Elliott Varner Smith for SBG. 4: SBG, courtesy of Oshkosh B'Gosh ; *ill.* Seth Larson. 5: *t.l.* Michael Medici/Sonlight Images for SBG; *t.r.* Courtesy, Delta Music *b.l.* Kugler/FPG International; *b.r.* Bob Daemmrich/Tony Stone Images. 6-7: Jody Jobe. 10-11: Cindy Salans Rosenheim. 12-13: Randy Verougstrate. 14-15: Eldon Doty. 16: *t.l.* Peter Lamberti/Tony Stone Images; *t.r.* Breck P. Kent/Animals, Animals; *b.l., b.r.* SuperStock; *ill.* Liisa Chauncy Guida. 17: Leo Monahan. 18-19: Benjamin Vicent. 20: FourByFive/SuperStock; *ill.* Rollin Richter. 21: Steve Bjorkman. 23: Tom Tonkin. 26: *t.l.* J. Traver/Gamma/Liaison; *t.r.* ©1989 Jack Vartoogian; *m.* Brown Brothers; *b.l.* Steve Vidler/Leo De Wys, Inc.; *b.r.* Mercury Archives/The Image Bank. 27: Liisa Chauncy Guida. 28: Jeff Nishinaka. 29: *boy* David Young-Wolff/Tony Stone Images; *girl* Rex Butcher/TonyStone Images. 30: courtesy of Oakview School, Nutley, NJ; *t.r.* David Young-Wolff/Tony Stone Images; *b.l.* Miguel A. Gandert for SBG. 32-33: Sandra Speidel. 35: *background*: Craig Tuttle/The Stock Market; *insets: t.* Elliott Varner Smith for SBG; *b.* Paul Barton/The Stock Market. 39: *streetcar courtesy of LTC (ret.)* Wm. G. Byrne, Jr. 40-41: Robin Hotchkiss. 42: Ron Thomas/FPG International; *ill.* Gwen Connelly. 44: Jackie Snider. 45: Olivia. 46-47: Gwen Connelly. 48-49: Winifred Barnum Newman. 50-51: Michael Radencich. 54: Steve Hickey. 54-55: *ill.* Lorraine Shirkus. 55: courtesy, The Morris Museum and FRIENDLY'S Ice Cream Shop, Convent Station, N.J. 56: *t.* Phil Borges/Tony Stone Images; *b.l.* Eve Arnold/Magnum; *b.r.* FPG International. 57: *t.l.* Ann Nielsen/Gamma Liaison; *t.r.* Elliott Varner Smith for SBG; *b.* Lori Adamski Peek/ Tony Stone Images. 59: Pamela Becker. 61: *t.l.* Obremski/The Image Bank; *t.r.* Lawrence Migdale; *b.* Elliott Varner Smith for SBG. 62: The Joffrey Ballet's production of THE NUTCRACKER, photo ©Herbert Migdoll; *ill.* Barbara Lambase. 64-65: Kat Thacker. 66-67: FOOTPRINTS AND SHADOWS by Anne Westcott Dodd. Illustrations by Henri Sorenson. ©1992. Used by permission of Simon & Schuster Books for Young Readers; *border ill.* Liz Conrad. 68: Elliott Varner Smith for SBG; *ill.* Doreen Gay Kassel. 69: Doreen Gay Kassel. 70-71: Doreen Gay Kassel. 74: Terry Powell. 75: Doreen Gay Kassel. 76: Doreen Gay Kassel. 77: Jack Graham. 79: Doreen Gay Kassel. 84: Geraldo Suzan. 87: Darius Detwiler. 88-89: Jack Graham.

Sound Bank Photos: 91: *Cabaca-* The Shrine to Music Museum/University of South Dakota; *Native American ankle bells-* The Mathers Museum.

"SALLY WALKER", Pastel by Brenda Joysmith, copyright 1987. All Rights Reserved.

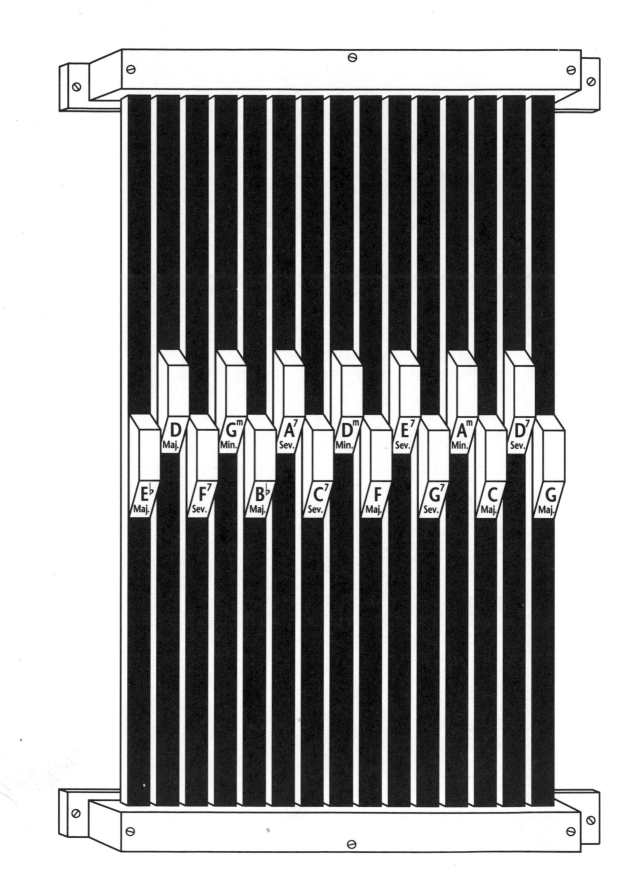